a family of
21 kids!

a family of
21 kids!

Living with 21 siblings

Written by

Regina Witherspoon

authorHOUSE®

AuthorHouse™
1663 Liberty Drive
Bloomington, IN 47403
www.authorhouse.com
Phone: 1-800-839-8640

Luralee Hylton, Aunt Nancy, Sally-Ann Johnson

Published by AuthorHouse   02/19/2013

ISBN: 978-1-4772-9792-6 (sc)
ISBN: 978-1-4772-9813-8 (e)

Library of Congress Control Number: 2012923286

Any people depicted in stock imagery provided by Thinkstock are models, and such images are being used for illustrative purposes only.
Certain stock imagery © Thinkstock.

This book is printed on acid-free paper.

This book is dedicated to someone I love
with all my heart and will miss forever
part of me is gone too soon.
I love you Mom . . .

A BIG FAMILY

21 kids born to Sally & John Witherspoon; both were born and raised in South Carolina. There were 9 boys (Billy, Mackey, Henry, Willie Jr., John & Johnny the twins, Steve, Sam, and Arthur) and 11 girls (JoAnn, Sally Ann, Mary, Geneva, myself, Elizabeth, Barbara, Carrie, Laura, Annette, and Cynthia). She had 1 miscarriage and 4 stepchildren (Stringbean, Toney, Ann, and Pearlie). She even raised two of her grandchildren; Betty and Danielle Witherspoon. We were all born at St. Raphael hospital in New Haven, CT. They knew my mom and dad so well they put her in the newspaper for having 21 kids. No C-section or drugs, my mom had us natural and out of all 21 she had one set of twins, but they didn't live for long. All my mother's children had a gift. Even if they didn't use it, it was still there. Almost everyone in our family was blessed with a talent. My grandma Irene, on my mom's side, had 19 children of her own. I don't know too much about her past. She died when I was little. My dad's mom only had 8 kids and he was the only boy. She may not be with us anymore but she's the one who gave life to the start of this generation. I know she looks down on us and I miss the talks we used to have. I didn't trust anyone but her. My parents basically grew up around each other working the same farm and going to the same school and church. He knew her family and she knew his very well.

My parents already had four kids born in the south before they moved to Connecticut. It's then when they moved there the journey of a big family began.

With this growing family dad had to find a job. Mom stayed at home with us. We only had one car. Mom had to dress the younger ones to walk with the older ones to school. This was her routine every morning. She couldn't leave us home by ourselves. We were too young. Whether it snowed or rained this was our walk to and from every day. Some say God gave my mom so many for a reason. I just don't understand what they meant by that. As we got older things started to change; the girls became teenagers and so did the boys. There were different mood swings, arguing, yelling at each other don't touch this or don't touch that. We had to share everything: bathrooms, beds, clothes, and shoes. We did get along very well though. It took a lot to make us mad at each other. I think if we didn't get along mom was going to get us anyway. We were living in the projects then. I remember this very well. Dad didn't let us do anything that much. He had this favorite chair he would sit in and watch TV. Mom would be walking around cleaning and singing while she cooked. Her big red glasses sat on her face as she walked. Her big mouth would open up and sing as if she was in church. I'm sitting down at the door of my room watching her. Oh how she would move her feet and clap her hands side to side. Looking back in my room my sisters were so into the TV, but not me! I stayed at the door in my room staring at mom. Boy! I could smell the food in the air can't wait to eat that good food lol. Now dad's sleeping, the TV's still playing. I could hear my brothers in their room talking and laughing. I peeked around my room to see what they were doing. They were playing Pac-man. I loved that game.

Looking towards the kitchen I could hear mom calling dad. "Buuuubba!" I moved back fast in the room so dad wouldn't see me. Then mom would go back to singing. My mom loved church. She was raised in it so she brought us up in it. When the church doors opened mom was there and so were we. Mom even had bible study with us at home. If anything she was going to make sure we had the word in us. There's nothing wrong with that. Some days we just wanted to go outside and dad wouldn't let us. We could hear the kids playing outside by our window. Since we couldn't go out we made up stuff to do to kill time like playing school and church. My little brother Henry was the preacher lol. We played house too. Sam made up a board game. He took a box and made it into a football field. He ripped up some papers in little pieces so we could use it for the game he made. We would blow the paper across the board trying to beat whoever was playing against us. We picked football teams and I was the dolphins. It was fun, it was something to do.

The only two places mom took us were church and school. That was it. The kids used to say our parents were so mean they wouldn't let us do anything. We just didn't pay them any attention. Getting ready for the school year was kind of scary. It was my first time going to school without my mom being around me. Just the thought of thinking about it; not even my sisters and brothers would be with me. Meeting other kids outside my family circle, how would that go? Would they like me? What would they think of me? Mom came in our room. "Put y'all clothes out for tomorrow," she said. "And go take y'all baths." She got my clothes together for the big day. My sisters were telling me their moments they had in first grade. "You're going to have a lot of fun," they said to me. Mom did my hair so she wouldn't have to do it in the morning.

The school wasn't far. It was across the field where we lived so mom didn't have far to walk us. It was time to go to bed now and mom told us to go to sleep so we could get up in the morning. I couldn't go to sleep thinking about tomorrow. Before I got up out the bed I wanted to make sure my sisters were asleep. I could hear mom and dad talking in the kitchen. Our door to the room was closed. I went to my window to look out. I could see a lot of boys standing outside smoking and drinking. I liked to look out at the stars and just stare at them wishing a lot of things. Smelling the fresh air and feeling the wind blow in my face gave me some type of calmness. After a while I climb back in my bed for the night. The next morning mom came in our room to wake us up. We had to move quickly so the boys could get to the bathroom too. I started to get butterflies in the bottom of my stomach. Everyone was ready an hour later. "It's time to go," mom yelled. We all started walking towards the front door. Mom held my hand as we walked, giving us that talk. She would say "Go to school and listen to the teacher. They already have their education now get yours. And don't be hard headed," giving us that eye to eye contact. We all knew what that meant for us; we were going to get it if we didn't listen in class.

THE BULLY

The school I went to was Clinton Avenue. My teachers name was Mrs. Gardner. Walking in the class I was so scared. The teacher looked at me and smiled. I didn't smile back because I didn't know what to think of her. She was a stranger to me. Her glasses hung low on her nose with a short haircut. I went to take a seat and mom looked at me. "Be good," she said. I shook my head saying ok. I didn't want my mom to leave me there but she left walking out the door. I was hoping she'd come back and get me. Mrs. Gardner shut the door and began to speak telling us what we were going to learn for the whole year. I sat next to a girl named Baby Carrie. I don't know why they called her that. I was thinking maybe she was the only child. After we did some work in class we started drawing and coloring and playing with paint. I was starting to like it after all but I still watched the door to see when my mom was coming to get me. Mrs. Gardner walked over toward me and whoever was sitting at my table and said "Its time to get ready for lunch," so we cleaned up. Baby Carrie brought her lunch to school. I asked her why she doesn't eat the lunch here. She said "Because I can't. My mom and dad would have to pay for it. They make too much money." "Ohhhh," I said and then she said "I don't eat what they have sometimes anyway."

Getting back in the classroom, our teacher asked us to remain in our seats while she stepped out the class for a minute. As soon as she did some kids got out their chairs and started walking around laughing and talking. I stayed where I was. I remembered what mom told us. Down the hallway you could hear my teacher's shoes. Everyone knew it was Mrs. Gardner walking down the hall headed back to class. The kids started running back to their seats. She came in looking around at us with those big glasses reminding me of my mother. When she looked at me she just smiled. I just stared at her. "Eventually I'll get used to you," I said to myself. It was almost time to go home and I couldn't wait for mom to come get me. I missed my sisters and brothers and dad too. She passed out our homework to us. I was happy to go home and do some work. Packing my book bag I was so happy to see mom. I had so much to tell her about my day. We walked down the hall to pick up Betty and Danielle, who were living with us. Walking back home mom asked us if we listened and we said yes. Soon after that we saw the others running up to us. I was so happy to see them and happy to tell them I had homework. As I was going to school I was getting used to it and mom had stopped walking us. The older ones would bring us to school before they went to their school. I was happy to go to school now.

I heard about a Christmas program for our school and I wanted to be a part of it. I asked my teacher about it and she said "When you go to music class mention it to the teacher and she'll talk to you about it." That would be nice to do. So the next day we went to music class. Walking in the room, I went right over to the music teacher and asked can I be a part of the Christmas program. She said "Let me hear you sing." I was shy but I did it. She looked at me as her eyes grew wide. Then she asked me was I related to these people she had named. I told her yes, they're my sisters and she said "I knew it! You all can sing. Yes, I would love for you to be a part of it," and she handed me a permission slip for mom to sign. I was hoping mom said yes. We started learning some Christmas songs. I loved music class: it was like singing at church. We headed back to our class and our teacher had cupcakes at the table with pizza and drinks.

Standing beside the table with all this good stuff were someone's parents. It was a boy in our class's birthday. They surprised him and wanted to celebrate it with his classmates. My day was getting better and better. It was the best day ever. Now it was time to help the teacher clean up and get ready to go home for the day.

The bell rang and I went out the classroom waiting for my sister Sally to come get us. There she was waving her hands at us to come on. Going out the door heading outside, we started walking home. As we were walking we saw my two sisters Carrie and Cynthia. Their school wasn't far from ours. Walking with them were two more girls. I thought they were their friends but one of the girls was picking with Cynthia. The other girl that was with her was laughing at everything this girl did. Looking at my sister's face I could tell she was so hurt by this and was scared to do anything about it. The girls followed my sister all the way home and then walked away when we were near our front door. When we were inside the house my sister told my mom about this girl. Mom said she would write a letter to the school. Then she told my sister, "And you tell your teacher about this girl." Mom also told us she would pray to God about it. When we got in the room, my sister didn't say anything to us. I knew she was hurting but I didn't know what to say to her. We just started doing our homework. Mom was making us something to eat. The older ones in high school came walking in the front door and the house went from silence to lots of noise. We told our sister Mary about this girl. She told us she would meet up with us tomorrow to see who this girl was that's picking with her. Our homework was done and we had to get ready for bible study. Mom made sure everything was done before we had to go. Clothes had to be out for the next day and homework had to be checked over. She even checked the room. We made sure the room stayed clean. If not, we would have had to deal with my mom and I didn't want that.

Walking out to the car, we were ashamed that people knew where we were going. They would yell out "Why y'all always going to church?" We just looked at them and said nothing. I didn't really want to go. I was missing my favorite shows on TV and I knew once we got back home it would be time for bed. Sitting in church was boring. Just hearing the preacher talk about what mom talked to us about at home. Why couldn't we study at home with our family? Mom kept looking at us to see if our eyes dropped. If so we were in big trouble. If we talked we were in big trouble. She wanted us to pay attention in the church. That was kind of hard to do as a young child. Getting back home I knew dad couldn't wait to get us out of this area. It wasn't bad he just didn't like when so many people smoke and drank. He didn't care about being around them. We were getting ready for bed. My brothers would walk in our room with some corny kind of a joke lol. We would tell them to get out. Laying down for bed again I waited for everyone to go to sleep. When it was quiet and I heard the snoring, I knew they were out like a bulb. I would go back to the window and stare again at the stars and feel the wind blow in my face. Some days I could smell the rain in the air. I left the window open because I liked to go to bed cold. It felt nice and cozy. I went back to bed and snuggled under the blankets.

When the morning came we got ready. Mom handed Cynthia the letter to give to the school and the teachers. "I will call them and talk to them." She then handed me my slip that she had signed. I was so happy! Walking to school that day I was happy. I couldn't wait to put it in my music teacher's hand. Things went smooth the whole day. We had to get ready for picture day. My concern was how mom was going to have me looking. The day went smooth and now it was time to go home. The bell rang and it seemed like the day went by so fast. Leaving out the classroom, my sister was standing there waiting for us. I was tired of hearing about this girl picking with her. We saw them coming and behind them there was that girl again messing with my sister. Carrie stopped them and told Cynthia to fight the girl. Me, Betty, and Danielle, kept looking towards the house to see if mom was standing at the door. I didn't want to get in trouble for this. My sister was scared to fight her. I'm like don't you want this girl to stop messing with you? My sister just walked away. She didn't want to fight. Since Mary saw this, she looked at the girl and said to her "Touch my sister again and you will have to deal with me. And go get your sister. I'm not scared of her either." The girl walked away and was like "Whatever, whatever." We walked away and started walking towards our house. It was like the teachers nor the school could do anything with this girl. She was just going to do what she liked best and that's picking with people. What she got out of it? I don't know I just think she was jealous or something or had some issues. I know my sister wanted this girl to leave her alone. Why my sister? No one knew why. I think it was because my sister showed fear. You don't want anyone to know you're afraid of them. That alone will give them a reason to pick with you because they know you won't say anything back. I can't speak for my sister because I don't know what she was dealing with inside her soul. No one should have to face this alone.

As the next morning arrived we were getting ready for school. I was hoping this girl would just leave and go to another school. Walking to school my sister was kind of quiet. I couldn't help but think about my sister all day in school. It was time to head home across the field. There were my two sisters but without the girl this time. We asked her where the girl was.

They told us they didn't know so we went home feeling happy she wasn't around this day. When we got home dad and mom were ready to take us out to the park. I was happy. I knew it was going to be fun. We stayed for the rest of the day. Later, when it got dark, we went back home and started taking baths. Mom and dad talked to us until it was time for bed telling us about their younger years and what they used to do. Our routine was always the same. We went walking to school the next day running late. The kids were waiting outside for the teachers to get them. I told my sisters good bye and they went on their way. We had so much to do. Our school tests and practice for the Christmas program. I was tired and couldn't wait to get home. Going to school and then some day's church . . . not complaining, just saying.

Sally didn't meet us this day so we started walking home. Carrie, Cynthia, and Mary walked towards us. They told us that the girl who was picking with Cynthia died. She skipped school with two other girls. There were so many different stories of that tragic day that you didn't know what to believe. One thing was certain; she was killed by a train. I felt so bad for her and her family. I wouldn't wish this upon anyone. It's just plain sad. I didn't know the girl to begin with but regardless of what she did I still felt sorry for her. My heart went out to her family. When we got home we explained it to mom. She was shocked, like wow. Later on that day the news was on. They were talking about what happened. We talked all night in the room feeling so sorry for this girl. The next day walking in our classroom our teacher told us to just take our seats. The class was waiting for her to talk. She started telling us about when someone dies. The kids were asking questions about death then on the loud speaker our principal said "We're going to have a moment of silence for the young lady who passed away." We didn't do any work in class. She just talked to us.

THE BIG MOVE

Mom and dad made the decision to move out of the projects to South Carolina. I didn't want to go to the South. I was so used to the city. I was kind of mad. Getting used to the South is not going to be easy and it didn't take long for my parents to find us a place to stay.

The place we moved to was just like the place we lived in the city just calmer. Mom started going to this church called Saint Paul Holiness. It was nice. They treated their youth with love. They had so many things for us to do, like movie night. I loved moving here. It was quiet and dry; no cars passing by with loud music, no sidewalks so you had to be careful walking the streets, everything was very far from each other, and there were more woods than anything. Dad had found a job and mom took care of us and the house. Going to church? Oh we was ready to go. Not saying this was the perfect place but there weren't as many crimes going on here like the city. We were having so much fun. Dad started going over to grandma's house to help out. Grandma was always happy to see us and my two aunts who still lived with grandma. One of my aunts was deaf and couldn't talk well. Grandma, she loved her sprite sodas lol and my two aunts used to always fuss at each other. Down the street from grandma dad had a sister. Her husband and their kids lived over there. It was a place for us to go. Our cousin Cathy, her brother and baby sister Debra, we started being close to each other. Every time we came around dad would let us go down to my aunt's house and we would sit over there and talk about anything. I remember when my parents had to go back to CT to do something and we stayed with my aunt MaryAnn. We would get dressed and out the door we'd go down the street to my other aunt's house. Their parents went with my parents so just their kids were home at the time.

Across from my aunt's house there was a boy and his little brother. Cathy brought us over there to meet them while they were talking. I had my eye on his little brother. We played tag and ran around his yard. I never felt this kind of feelings for anyone; I didn't know where they were coming from. My body was hype and my heart pounded as fast as can be. I didn't want him to see me looking at him so hard so I would look other places when he looked at me. I had this smile on my face that I couldn't get rid of. When it was time for us to leave I didn't want to leave him. It felt like I lost something valuable of mines. We went back to my cousin's house and I sat down. Now he was on my mind and I couldn't get him out. I never told my sisters about it. They would have teased me and embarrass me in the front of him so I kept it to myself. You couldn't tell me anything. I wanted to make sure I looked nice and my hair was done right. We started going over to their house a lot. I didn't know how I was going to pull this off when my parent's got back because they wouldn't approve of me playing around with a boy.

A BROKEN HEART

One morning we went down early to my cousin's house. She was awake and we had just ate breakfast I don't know why my cousin gave my sister Mary the keys to my uncles car but she did. Me, Carrie, and Cynthia jumped in the car with her. She started driving and we were jumping up in the back seat, something we knew not to do in dad's car. We were at the end of the road and she took a turn. We went into the ditch! I was scared so I jumped out on my side to make sure they were alright. My cousins came running asking if we were ok. We were trying to figure out how we'd get this car out of the ditch. We finally got help and towed the car out and put it back where my uncle had it at. Cathy was laughing so hard and so were we. It was too funny. She also put the keys back. The good thing about it was the car wasn't messed up. Thank God. When my parents came back from the city we were scared. My aunt and uncle didn't say anything about the car though.

My cousin Cathy had 3 boys; Maurice, Dewayne, and Leroy. Leroy was the youngest and I loved holding him lol. We still went down to my aunts like we used to and I was still playing with my new friend. I even started having dreams about him. I was starting to feel crazy, couldn't even control my emotions. But I made sure things didn't get out of hand. Mom helped around grandma's house. Dad cleaned the yard took out the trash. We helped some times when we were needed but other than that we went back down to my cousin's house. My friend's brother liked my sister. They would talk and walk. We would just play around until dad would call for us to leave for the day. I couldn't wait to get back to grandma's house tomorrow. As the night went and morning arose, we were ready to go. This time I knew we were going to be over there for a while because mom was going to cook for them. That gave me more time to play.

When we arrived at grandma's, mom asked us for some help so it took a good couple of minutes until we could play. Finally we were finished. We started walking down to my aunt's house. This time I didn't see Mary at the boy's house so when we got near them I asked "You're not going over there?" She said "They left. They took a trip so they'll be gone for the whole weekend." I was so sad because I wanted to see his face and that smile. It was raining Monday morning but my parents still went over to Grandma's. My cousin came over to get us and we begged mom to let us go down to auntie's house. I wanted to be there so when my friend came home I could tell him I missed him. I don't know why but a deep part of me wanted to tell him badly how I felt about him. I was just too scared to explain it to him.

We were talking under my cousins shed and to my surprise here they were, driving into their parking lot. Mary went over there first and she didn't take long to come back. I saw the look on her face and I had looked over and saw the boy but not his brother. When she came back to the shed she spoke in a slow voice and said "He told me his brother died over the weekend. He drowned." My heart started hurting. It felt like someone shot me right in it. I couldn't breathe. I kept asking myself how could this be? I blamed myself for everything. I just wanted to tell him how I felt about him and I blew any chances I had to tell him. I wanted to go home, lay in my bed, and no one bother me. I was sad that whole day but I kept a smile on my face because I didn't want anyone to know how I felt and how it was hurting me. Finally getting home, I went to the bathroom and fixed my bath water. I let all my tears out. Why'd this have to hurt me so bad? I cried in silence for a minute while I was sitting in the water. I begin to wonder why I was like this, what was going on with me. I told myself I would never go in a pool or near a pool in my life again. I was so mad at what happened to him. I wish I would have just talked to him. I will miss him so much.

THE CRAZY TEACHER

It took a while for me to get over losing someone I cared so much about. Why's my mind going crazy and why'd my heart have to ache? Time went by and it was now time for my parents to enroll us in school. I didn't know if I was going to like it. Seeing new faces all over again . . . I wasn't too sure about that. We had everything we needed for our first day. We walked into the building and the kids were waving and saying hi. Some stopped to tell us their names, asking which teacher I had. "I don't know," I said. "I'm new here," and they would go "Ooooooh." Mom said to us again "Listen to the teacher y'all," and we'd say ok. I walked into my classroom and the kids looked at me so hard their eyes could've popped out from their faces. They were all nice and very friendly. They'd come up to me asking me questions about where I came from. I started wishing the same thing I did when I first started school, that mom would come get me. The teaching was totally different down here and the kids were a whole lot nicer than they were in the city. I wasn't trying to compare but there was a big difference in the two. The teacher was nice at first. But things started to get out of hand a few weeks later. The kids wouldn't listen to her at all. They was making her mad when she saw my brother henry she said to him tell your mother that your sister would not listen in class today. I was so shocked! Like OMG . . . you're kidding me right?! I didn't do anything wrong and of course when we got home he hand my mom the letter. She read it and boy oh boy did I get in some deep trouble. I tried to tell mom this lady was lying on me but mom didn't believe me. She said she'd believe an adult before she believed anything that came out of our mouths.

I didn't want to go back to school the next day. The teacher looked at me with an evil face when I walked in the classroom door. I wanted to go up to her and just slap her but I know I would get in trouble. I didn't want to deal with that so I did what I was told. We went outside and some of the kids wanted to go elsewhere when she yelled "Time to go back in. Let's go!" They took forever getting in line and as soon as we got back into class she did it again. "Heads on the desk until you all can understand when I say something I mean it." I was so pissed off because I knew she was going to lie on me again and boy was I right! She did. My brother shook his head and looked at me. I was thinking . . . mom said God answers prayers so I'm going to pray for God to show mom this teacher was lying. I never did anything to her for her to treat me like this. Who could I trust when no one listens? Walking home I cried. When I got in the door mom looked at me and said "You're going to get it. I told you to listen to that teacher." I felt so angry I was giving myself a headache I thought my blood was boiling inside, my eyes were so red.

Going to church took my mind off wanting to slap this teacher. I was glad when the school year came to an end. On the last day I though what should I do at the end of the year? Write her a long nasty letter and curse her out? Or do something else . . . . Then she'd be telling the truth about something I really did. I was already mad being in the south and now you provoked me to go off on you. I don't think we would all want that. The church we were going to had activities for us to be a part of so we were always on the go. My sister Mary had a baby and moved down after she was born. Her name is Lapreia. Since my sister had a baby she found a job and everyone around the house would help out with my niece. Her father and grandma lived in our area where they would come to see her as much as they could. When she would work he had the baby but my sister didn't want the baby to go with him without her being around. I don't blame her. A real mother is always concerned about their child. A lady from the church was so intrigued by my mom that she began talking to her about what she was going through.

One day she and her kids came over to our house to talk to mom. I was in the back room but close enough to the front to hear them talk. She was telling my mother about the blessings and doors that opened for her. She then started telling my mom about her daughter's teacher and how she treated her daughter. When she mentioned the school my eyes opened and I was hoping she didn't have the same teacher I had. She said this lady would call her and say her daughter did this and did that. She goes on to say "I got on my child about this but deep down inside I knew something was wrong. She was crying telling me she didn't do anything the teacher said. When my child cries I know she's telling me the truth." "One day I didn't tell my child I was coming to the school because I wanted to watch what was going on. I didn't tell the teacher I just popped up. I waited for class to begin and I peeked through the window and lay low where my daughter nor the teacher could see me. She was teaching them, they were answering some questions she asked, and then she gave them some class work. Some kids were raising their hands to get some help she walked over to them." She went on to say "After they were finished they went over their work together. She started talking again telling them what they were going to learn for the next two weeks in class. These kids were doing everything she claimed they weren't but there were two boys she had to keep speaking to. They would not listen to her at all. They went to recess and everything was fine there. She took them to lunch. That was good but 40 minutes before class was over she made them put their heads on the desk. I waited for the bell to ring and after the bell rang I walked in the classroom. The kid's heads were still on the desk. She walked up to me and told me all these things my child did and I'm like are you for real? I watched you all day with my child. You told me she was doing all this stuff and my poor child was looking at me ready to defend herself. I walked to the principal's office and talked to them and explain what happened. They took my child and changed her class." I wanted them to get rid of that teacher. I heard my mom say "My child had that same teacher," and then she said to the lady "You know why I didn't believe my child? Because I know kids like to lie to get out of trouble." I know my mom was sad about this teacher lying to her but she said sorry to me. I felt better now; God answered my prayer.

BACK TO THE CITY

Now that all this stuff was going on, my sister and her boyfriend were coming to visit us. My oldest sister Laura and her husband Earl would come down and take pictures, video tape everything inside and out, and anything we did around the house. We had fun when they came around. They came down and left. Mom and dad found a job after all the kids were in school. I was going to another school now and I was in a higher grade. I was doing great at school. One morning, getting ready for breakfast in the lunch room, I started to itch and it kept getting more and more annoying. My teacher sent me to the nurse's office. She called my house and told them I had the chicken pox. My sister Sally-Ann came to get me because dad and mom were working. We had to walk back home but it wasn't far. I hated the chicken pox. They made me mad, I got no rest, and the itch was getting the best of me but after a couple of days they went away. A couple of years after this my parents told us we were moving back to the city. I don't know why we were doing all this moving. I just got used to these schools and we had to move again, but I was happy to go back to the city. I missed it. My sister Mary and her daughter moved back too.

When we got to the city we moved from here to there. We finally got an apartment. Under us were my cousin Fred and his wife Rosalind. Next to them were my two sisters and brother. My sisters Sally Ann and Mary had babies on the way. This would be Mary's second child. While we lived in this area mom would take us to visit our uncle Danielle Lee. He lived in a nursing home. These old folks scared me when I would walk through the hallways. They would try to touch us or tell us to come to them. When we got to my uncle's room, he was sitting in the chair. We spoke to him. We sat in the chairs they had in his room looking at his TV. Mom asked him "How do you feel?" Sometimes she would read him the bible or sing. She'd even ask him if he remembered the things they used to do when they were younger. If mom had never brought me here I wouldn't have known who he was.

He and mom looked just alike. I didn't know too much of my mom's family but the others did. The only thing I remembered was their names. We weren't around them much, well the ones that were still living. The only two I knew well were Aunt Nancy and Aunt Ruth Moore.

We went to visit my uncle every day. Mom used to bring him food sometimes. Some days we wanted to go and some days we didn't. The people that lived next door to us were nice. They had four girls; Marsha, Jamie, Shanelle, and Candance. Playing in that back yard, those were the days. I will never forget kickball and double-dutch. Fred's dog chased Danielle all the way up the stairs. That day was so funny. Mom used to cook and give us bologna and rice. Being from the south, that's what they did. When mom's back turned I'd throw the bologna up to the ceiling and it would stick for a minute or so. I was hoping it wouldn't fall on mom's head. My sisters and brothers were silently laughing where mom couldn't hear them. When she moved to go into the room the bologna fell down. It was my first time doing this but it definitely wasn't my last.

Every day, as long as no one was fussing or fighting, dad let us go outside to play. One of the girls next door was going with my younger brother. She was so nice and funny. Just seeing them together was so cute and he treated her like a queen. She knew she had it good and she went to church with us every now and then. The church my aunt once had was now turned over to another pastor: Elder brooks. He was real nice to us. The people that were raised up around us, we called them family. Dealing with someone else being bullied by someone in church was just plain wrong. I stayed beside her because I knew her all my life. Anyone who would come in the church and try to bully someone had some serious issues. She told my mom a lot of things about me. No matter what she said I stayed friends with her. Even though I was kind of mad mom believed her, it was ok. I just got in trouble that's all. I didn't care at all, I stood by her side.

We got back home from church and Shanell came to get us to go outside. She just know how happy we were to have her around. Because of her, we were able to go out and play. Mom and dad used to come out and watch us play some times. My sisters would bring their kids out too. One day my cousin Lestine came over to fight Marsha. I think it was because of something she said. Dad just told us to come in. He never liked being around drama. This changed a lot of things. I remember when we moved into this nice apartment. It was much better than the last; no noise and no fighting was going on. We were finally in a quiet neighborhood. Our landlord downstairs had kids our ages. We hadn't met them yet. My parents would take us to the park. There were only 8 kids left in my mom's house. Mary was married, Geneva was married, and Lulu was married. I guess you could say some of the boys were everywhere.

FUN TIMES WITH MOM

The main park we went to was called Edgewood Park. My sisters and their families would meet us out there. Mom would make sandwiches and lots of other food to take with us. When we got there we started off playing baseball so we had to make teams. Mom threw the ball and dad would catch it. We hated it sometimes because dad and mom working together were too good for us. They would strike some of us out. Some of us were able to hit the ball and just barely make it home. We had people watching us like it was a real game. You heard yelling and some screaming "Go go go!" while my sister recorded us. When it was my turn, I took off my shoes. I ran faster without them. I was ready to hit, run, and bring my team home. Mom was fast with her hands and dad would catch any fast ball that came his way. My heart pounded and my hands shook but I kept my eyes focused on the ball. When she threw it at me I hit it up in the air. You could hear the people on the side saying, "Run girl, run!" That girl could hit. I took off as fast as I could. The rest of my team ran too. I made it to 3rd base. This was fun. We did this all day every day but we would stop to eat something. Mom would share our food with others that were in the park that day. The ice cream truck would come and dad would give us some change out of his pocket. We'd run to that truck. We stayed at the park until the sun went down for the day. Then, we'd pack our things and head home. We relaxed until it was time to go to bed. My parents would play spades with us to kill time, even checkers or Pac-man. No one could beat me at that game. They would tell us about things they used to do when they were younger.

One thing mom tried to do was get me to drink milk. I just couldn't drink it. I don't know why but it wouldn't go down and I'd have to run to the bathroom to throw it up. I still can't drink milk now. My stomach wouldn't allow me.

We went to another park and started to play baseball again. We called this park the Doo-Doo park. People would walk their dogs, let them use the bathroom, and leave the mess. Thank God no one sat in that park. They only walked their dogs. When it was my turn to hit, boy did I hit. I hit the ball so hard it broke one of the windows of the building in front of us. Mom yelled "Ruuuuuuun," and we ran to the car and took off that day. It was so funny. I think I hurt my stomach from laughing so much.

Now since I'd been going to schools in the south it was time I went to schools in the city. Like I said, it was very different when it came to dealing with the kids. Up north, if you didn't dress like them or if you were quiet you were a target for them to mess with. I never had problems with the kids in the south. I wasn't going to have anyone pick with me and I didn't say anything back. I had very few friends. Mom had us wearing dresses to school. She didn't believe in pants at that time so the cold days were painful days. The kids used to ask "Why do you wear skirts all the time?" I didn't want to tell them my mom didn't believe in wearing pants. I was happy when school was let out for the day. Mom used to go over to my aunt's house to see her. They would talk like sisters do. We'd get together with my cousin's and sing and make up songs. Our cousin Priscilla was the leader in our group. She used to teach us different keys to harmonize together and it came out beautifully. We'd make up silly songs; Wash It Out With Clorox, Lord Don't Let That Girl, Geneva Rump Cuss, McDonalds Is All I Eat, and Coca Cola.

After all this my cousin told us she wanted us to sing for a pastor who had asked her to sing at an event. We went with her one night but it was so long ago I forgot how we got to this event. When we got up to sing, the church was so shocked to hear us. They couldn't believe how great we sounded. Since then, we started singing for him at a lot of his events. My mom started going to his church which was located in Waterbury. My dad had a van. He would drive us but never came in the church. There were a few members at this church including his wife, their two boys, her mother, sister, and her brother. We were the youth of the church. He started asking my mom to sing and of course she called us to background her. When mom gets the microphone she didn't know when to stop lol. She helped them with selling things to put towards things for the church. She was very kind.

SAINTS OF THE CHURCH . . .

Everyone who tasted mom's food fell in love with it. A year or so after we joined, the pastor got another building. It was nice and much bigger. More people started to come. Since then, it began to grow more and more. We gained a youth choir and an adult choir. We had a down stairs and we'd eat there between the break from Sunday school and morning service. He wanted us to sing so much he made people in the church mad. Trust me, we didn't care. Coming from New Haven going to Bridgeport during the week was hard. Getting up for school wasn't working. I only wanted to go on Sunday. Mary, Sally, and their kids joined the church. My aunt Ruth and her kids were there as well. So were other family members. It was better because there were more youth.

One thing I didn't like was when the pastor asked for all the ministers to come up and pray for people. A lot of them were trying to get to the first lady and didn't want my mom to touch them and pray for them. Isn't God in everyone? That's what I believed. It was ok though. Mom didn't care at all. I was already having problems in school and dealing with these people at church just made me want to stay home. Mom cooked dinner one Saturday afternoon and invited some people from the church. My sister Cynthia was dating the drummer. His name was James. He and his mother came. We had to go pick them up from the train station. The pastor, his wife, and other members from the church came down too. They were enjoying themselves. Mom cooked everything that day. We were close to the pastor and his wife.

The first lady of the church always talked on a mother to daughter level. I wasn't sure about telling her about things. I didn't know if she would have told my mom. One Sunday she gave me her number to call her so we could talk. At first mom told me "Don't do it. She already has a lot to deal with plus two small children." So, when she asked "Why didn't you call me?"

I told her "Mom said I shouldn't mess with you." "No," she said. "I want you to call me. I'm ok." One Monday afternoon I called her and we started talking. She would give me some bible verses to read and after we talked for a while, she would end the call with a prayer. I was getting used to it but I still wasn't sure about telling her how I felt about school and the issue I was having. I just wasn't ready to open up that far yet.

Early the next morning, after the bell rang, I left. I knew my brother Sam, my niece Betty, and nephew Danielle were already gone. I was thinking, trying to come up with an excuse as to why I was coming home late. These two girls were following me. I was ready to fight if I had to. They followed me all the way to the top of the hill. I wanted them to get a little closer but they didn't; they just turned away. I don't know why she didn't like me. You don't know me and I don't know you. We've never talked to each other so what was your problem? When I got home mom said "Where you was at?" I told a lie to get out of it and it worked. I didn't want to tell her the real reason. She would have said "Stop running your mouth. No one was gonna mess with you." With these kids trouble always seemed to come to you. Before I let anyone boss me around I'd rather get in trouble at home. Finished with everything, I would call the first lady to talk to her to ease the stress. I use to call her without mom knowing.

After church on Sundays, mom would have all this food laid out in the kitchen; cornbread, mac & cheese, collard greens, baked ham, banana pudding, cakes, and homemade sweet tea. I loved Sunday's! I remember when she'd make peanut butter and jelly sandwiches.

She would stir it together then put it on the bread. When she made up her mind to go back to the south I stayed with one of my sisters and her husband. That's when things got crazy and people at the church started showing their true colors. I stopped calling everyone I guess they was thinking they can take my parents spot, oh no. I'd respect you as long as you respected me. This girl and her grandma joined the church and all hell broke loose. She would start trouble with us. I wasn't paying her any attention and all of a sudden my name was all up in things. She told the pastor me and another girl wanted to jump her. I don't need anyone to help me fight a person if it's only that one person. Why she said this, I didn't know. He called us to his office and just went off on us. Even an officer would have asked us our side of the story to see what was going on. He didn't ask so I started going crazy. After that, when he would preach I closed my ears and when he said stand I stayed seated. I was pissed off. I know it was wrong but I just wanted him to hear our side of the story that's all.

I knew he was calling me the devil but it was all good. I didn't care. Everyone tried to have a say in it. I say they were provoking me. We've never been on the same level since then. They spoke when they wanted to and so did I. I had a lot of problems with these churches. They're more to handle than the people in the streets but I was good. I didn't have to answer to anyone but God. Hurting someone with the truth is better than making them happy with a lie. I couldn't put it any better than that. I was learning how to handle things better though. I wasn't perfect and neither were they. Someone told a friend who asked me to be her kids Godmother she couldn't do it because in order to be a Godmother you have to be saved. I was shocked to hear who it came from. I knew why she said it. It's funny how people can change so quickly. Remember this; what comes around goes back around. After hearing that, I called my mom to ask her if it was true and I told her who it came from. The words of wisdom she gave me made me feel so much better.

I still went to the church because my sister was still there. Sitting in the window while the snow fell, I'd began thinking about the times when the holidays came around and how mom would have all this food on the table. She would cook all day Christmas Eve. She would stay up till a certain time in the morning and then she would stop and get maybe 2 or 3 hours of sleep before everyone started to come over. She had to make sure the house was cleaned; bathrooms, rooms, and walls. She wanted it perfect. We were so tired. All this for one day was a mess. It was too much. She had us working so hard but only on these days. We did this every other Saturday as well. I remember when she didn't have the car because dad drove it to work. She would fill the tub up half way with water and put the clothes in. Then we would trump the clothes, walking back and forth in the tub for a while. When it was time to come out she'd hand us a towel to dry our feet. Then, she would finish the clothes by ringing the water out. Our feet looked white as could be. It was fun and I loved doing it but I miss those days. There was snow falling, Christmas songs playing, making up the 12 days of Christmas, and my sister Laura recorded everything there. There wouldn't be another Christmas like it. Having fun with each other would never be the same but the moments would always remain to look back on.

GENERATIONAL CURSE

One thing I can say about my family . . . . there were a lot of secrets from generation to generation being kept within the families. One example was molestation and rape of other family members. This happened more than once in mine. Why was it so hard for them to go to someone who would willingly be with them? Why couldn't they accept the word no? I just don't get it. I thank God I wasn't one of them but I do speak for the ones that it happened to. For anyone in the world going through this, you shouldn't have to face it alone. I think no one would speak up because they thought they were going to start a war in the family. You are a human and no means no. I don't care who you are. If you don't want to talk about it, it's ok. Just whisper to God and he will help you. I know it's hard to trust again. Now I see why mom kept us by her side and never let us go anywhere without her. We never stayed nights at anyone's house. When she was younger, she got raped and that's how JoAnn was born.

Why so many? I wish the world would speak more on this issue something needs to be done. I wondered how someone could go on without talking to that person or asking them for forgiveness. How could you overlook hurting another family member, acting like it never happened or they lied about it? All I'm saying is things could have turned out another way. I know we all were young when this happened but only God knows what really went on in that room. I'm not trying to start up nothing or step on toes, I'm just being real. What if it was your child and someone in your family touched them. How would you respond to it? The problem is no communication and people pointing fingers. Look at it this way; they were fine until it happened.

My sister was a normal little girl but all that changed one weekend going to an event not far from home. She came back a different person and that's when everything started to take a down fall for her. She had to change schools and was in out of certain places. My sister has been through a lot. One thing that made me mad was how people would talk about it. All I could say was put yourself in her shoes. Then tell me what you thought about it. Some of them couldn't go to sleep at night because someone was trying to mess with them while they slept. We shouldn't have to fight to protect our bodies when were supposed to be family. My sister couldn't go to the high school we were going to. She had to go somewhere else to finish school.

High school was totally different. Girls looked like grown woman, make-up, high heels, tight pants, short shirts, everything you could think of. I thought you were only going to school to learn and get an education not to try and get the boys to stare. "If they don't like what they see without you having to look like that they're not good for you," mom used to say. One time dad came to pick us up. We would run to the car so fast so no one would see us getting into the car. We were ashamed of my dad's car. I think it was more of us thinking they would tease us than anything. As kids you never knew what kids could come up with. It was like that in our days. I can imagine what they do now that each generation becomes wiser. There are things I only wish I could have done over but don't want to go back to. Now I see why mama said to enjoy our lives and not try to grow up so fast. As I become older, I saw a lot of things life had in store for me. I wasn't ready for what lie ahead of me.

I LOST MY SISTER

One day I remember clearly was the year of the Freddy Fixer parade. Me and a couple of friends bought new outfits for that day. We walked around looking into the crowd to see who we knew or who was in the parade. It was already hot. The sun was beaming brighter and brighter as the day went by. Later on that night, I stayed at one of my friend's house in Waterbury. I wanted to get away for a while. Late evening I was sitting in her kitchen watching her cook and her phone rang. It was my cousin Priscilla so I took the phone to see what she wanted. She was talking so soft. I could barely hear her but I knew whatever she was trying to say wasn't good. She told me my sister Elizabeth passed away. She was hit by a car. "Huh????" I said in a shocked voice. She said "We can come and get you if you want us to," and I told her "Yes."

Looking around in the bathroom I just started to cry. Wow, my sister's really gone. I didn't know how to react or what to think. How did a car hit her? I was so out of it. Now I couldn't wait to go home and find out the whole story. When I got back home, getting out of the car I could smell the rain in the air. I began to wonder if that saying is really true; every time someone dies, it rains because I just found out this news and it started to rain. I asked my sisters what happened. They said she went to the emergency room because her head was hurting. She had a tumor growing in her brain. The doctor gave her some medicine to ease the pain. They told her they wanted her to stay overnight to monitor her but she didn't want to stay. She signed herself out. She started walking towards her daughter Tarshia's house. As she started walking she went to cross the street. A policeman was speeding and he hit her. He hit her so hard she was thrown to the next street. When she landed, all the bones in her body broke and one of her toes came off. When they took her body to the hospital they didn't know who she was. They were calling her Jane Doe until a nurse that knew one of my sisters called her and told her what happened. The officer had left the scene but they found him.

Now that the whole family knew what had happened, it was time to mourn and lean on each other for support. I knew this hurt Tarshia more than any of us. This was her mother. Elizabeth wasn't only a mother, she was a grandma as well. Tarshia only had two children at the time; Natasjah and Tasheem but my sister was a proud grandmother. One thing she wasn't afraid to do was speak her mind. Whether you liked it or not she was going to say how she felt. After her funeral the funeral home gave her daughter this nice teddy bear. I thought it was so cute. I'm going to miss my sister. I called mom later on that week to see how they were doing. She told me how Elizabeth called her and wanted to sing with her and told how she wanted to come down and see her but no one would help her. She wanted to see mama so bad. "Did she ask someone," I asked. She said "Yea, she did." I knew then my sister knew something was going to happen. She didn't know what it was and wanted to see mom one last time. It hurt me so bad. I wish she could have seen mom before this happened to her. My half-sister Pearlie was murdered too. They never found who killed her. The case just went cold. We never heard the police say anything about it after that.

GOD IS GOOD

I have to share this miracle with you and it comes with pain and the loss of love all at the same time. My oldest sister Laura was the best mother, daughter, wife, aunt, and grandmother she could be. She met her husband Earl at a club when they were younger. Not too long after they started dating, they go married. They had 3 kids; Jason, Jermaine, and Javon. My sister was a hard working woman who cared about her family and her wellbeing. She was just like my mom. She stayed in church. She was on the church choir and the usher board. She even sung with us. She kept herself busy in the church. She only allowed us to see the happy part of her but deep down inside she was facing problems she had kept to herself for a while. She talks to me about it now. Her son Jermaine was the oldest and he had a little girl named Jaylah. My sister poured so much love on her. She loved her as if she were her own child. She came down every summer and made sure to see her mom when she had her vacations. Earl came with her and would bring his best friend with them.

Laura was loving and caring. She took care of Elizabeth's funeral when she passed. I remember her always recording us singing songs we'd make up and then she'd take it to her job to let them hear. Her co-workers loved hearing us sing all the time. She made so many recordings of the family she could have made a movie. One night I was watching TV. I went into the kitchen to get something to drink and the phone rang. Someone was calling my mom and telling her that Lulu was missing. Mom said "She's somewhere. Maybe she will come around." The next day one of my sisters called to check on mom. Mom asked about Lulu and she said she was fine. She's at a hotel for now. All this happened a week before her life took a turn for the worst. The last time she talked to mom, she was fussing about something that had happened. That was the last time we heard from her. It made mom mad and upset but she was alright about it.

Everything happened one night so quickly. She and her youngest son went to bible study in Bridgeport, CT. She came from New Haven. After church was over I was told she went into the back of the church and was reading something they had back there. All of a sudden she just fell straight down. Someone ran to the back to see what had happened. When they get to the back of the church she wasn't responding. They called 911 and she was rushed to the hospital. She had to be recessitated. The doctors discovered she had 2 strokes and an aneurysm on 1 side of her brain. When we heard the news everyone was shocked. We couldn't believe it. "She was just down here," my father said. My face was still frozen. I didn't know what to think of it.

The next morning while we were packing some things to take with us the phone rang again. Someone was telling my mother they were thinking about pulling the plug on my sister.

With an upset voice mom said, "Tell them don't do nothing until we get there!" After hanging up she turned to me and said "I wish I knew the pastors number so I could call him." The number came to me and we called him. Mom told him not to let anyone pull the plug on her daughter until we got there. We left out so quickly. Everything was happening so fast. All I could think about was my sister and the last time she was down here. She complained about her head and the pain that would hurt her so bad. All she did was put her head down to rest on the table.

As we were riding, I was hoping she still looked like herself. Hmm, what would she look like? Would she be up and talking? We finally got there and went straight to the hospital. We went up to the I.C.U and entered the waiting room area. There were a couple of people there already. My mom and dad went in first to see her. Then my brother Sam and I waited to go see her. When we finally went in I looked at my sister. She was hooked to so many things. She was a shade darker and her face was swollen but I knew it was her. I stared at her for a minute feeling scared. As I looked around her room many thoughts came to my head. How did her youngest son take this? We didn't see him because he was with my brother in-law. They had already left for the night. I went back into the room and I told mom "She looks different." She said "Yea, look what just happened to her. That's why."

Everyone was coming down every day to be by her side. The waiting room would be packed with family and friends. Some days would be good but some days were not. People came showing out and things got crazy. It didn't make any sense. We were there for my sister, so I thought. Mom never left Laura's side. She stayed at the hospital and I went home with one of my other sisters to get some sleep. My brother in-law Earl made sure dad ate something and they brought food up to mom. Mom said to us "She's gonna make it." I told her if she could hear me squeeze my hand and she did. That gave me some hope.

The doctors were in denial. They were saying things but we didn't pay them any mind. I was wondering, at this point, how she was going to be once she got better. Talking with family and friends and having fun took some of the thoughts out of my head. One of my sister's friends from her job was there and he was telling us about the songs she let him hear. He was laughing and he was telling us how much fun they had when they were working. Her co-workers sent flowers, cards, and many other things, making sure they poured love towards her. Her husband and children came down crying in the waiting room. Mom told them "Don't cry. She will be ok." I just couldn't cry because I was still confused about the whole thing. I still didn't know much about what was going on and I still wondered what caused this.

A couple of days later it was time for us to head back down south. Laura still wasn't awake. When we got back, we had to tell the rest of the family what was going on. Our family up north kept calling mom to keep her updated. Not long after we'd got back, we got a call that she woke up. They put her in a nursing home for a while until my second oldest sister got her. One summer she brought her down and Laura didn't want to go back with her. My parents took over her care and she's still with us to this day. Her youngest son, Javon, stayed with us too. Her mind was not the way it used to be. She couldn't walk so we had to help her around. Her husband came down once since she's been down here with us and he never came back to see her again. That made me mad. All the years they spent together and he basically just threw her away. Your vows said for better or worse and she needed you more than ever at this point. It was ok though. We were all the love and support she needed.

I think the biggest part of her progress was love from her family. There was no support and none of them were by her side. It was sad. Mom and I were looking at some pictures of Laura one night while dad was watching TV. She looked sick and fake in some of them. She might have been in pain in these because she looked so different. Mom said "I told her to go to the doctors and let them check her out." I couldn't help but think that maybe this wouldn't have happened she would have been ok but I'm glad she made it out alive. Some pictures I would let her see to see if she remembered any of them. She remembered some of them but when it came to others she'd start asking, "Who is that?" When we said the names she'd say "Oh yea." No one knew what the future had in store for her. Her life was an example of how fast things could change. We see it happen every day from children to adults but we choose to ignore it until it happens to us. By then it's too late. She would ask about her kids every day but I didn't know what to tell her. "You only get one mother and one father so cherish every moment," I said. She would look at me with a smile on her face and say, "Right." Then she'd laugh. I had to remind myself that she wasn't the same person she was years ago. She could've lost her life.

Now that she was living with my parents it seemed like everyone had something to say about what needed to be done. When she was in Connecticut they had the chance to do it. Now that someone else was taking care of her, they wanted to feel like they were in charge. Bottom line; my mom raised 21 kids so I'm pretty sure she's capable of taking care of her daughter. It amazed me how people would talk. God has control of everything and he has the final say. You're not a nurse or a doctor and until you showed you had some type of license we didn't have to listen to you. Until then, you could take your advice and keep it to yourself. The truth is the truth and no one liked to hear it.

So many pastors told her she would walk again. I believed she would but without her family by her side how could she have faith to do so?

To me, it seemed she gave up on herself. I stared at her sometimes while she watched TV. I knew she wished she could see her sons a lot more than she did. She got excited when she saw them come around. She would be so happy and wasn't able to stop smiling. Her whole world changed. She went from doing everything for herself to needing everything done for her. This would depress any one. Your husband's out somewhere doing his own thing when you need him most and doesn't call once. Years passed by and all the money she had in her account was stolen from her. She doesn't even know what happened to it. All the years she saved and banked only to have it stolen from her. Her dreams were shattered so quickly before her eyes. I know she will walk again in due season. Her family needs to help her and give her some encouragement and support. I think that would make so much of a difference. Everyone likes to know there's at least one person who believes in them.

SHE LOST A LEG

I think mom's body was so tired from having so many kids. Every year she was pregnant. She wasn't letting her body rest as much. When people would do her wrong and talk about her she would say, "All I'm going to do is pray for them." She would leave everything in God's hands even her kids. Even when we were adults, mom still cooked for us. Certain people didn't like that but that was just mom. We tried to tell her we could do it but she didn't like people telling her what to do or how to do. I guess her motherly ways never went away. She always did for herself no matter what. Even if she was sick, she'd find a way to help herself. If I had to choose a role model, it would be her. I felt like if she could go through all that she went through and still be strong, so could I. I could move on with a smile on my face.

When my mom was younger, we would go to church revivals. One day we were at one of the revivals. They had it under a tent. She was walking, not paying attention. One of the spikes they used to hold the corners of the tent down wasn't hammered all the way in. Her foot snagged across it and she hurt her ankle really bad. We told her to go to the doctor but like always she said, "I'll be alright." It never really healed and I think this is what started the infection. We never thought it would cause her to lose her leg. Long before that she was diagnosed with diabetes. She had it for 30 years. Everyone would keep me updated on her condition and what was going on with her. She never wanted to go to the doctor. I don't know why but everyone has their reason for the things they do. She always prayed for herself and knew God would answer her. We were concerned about her and Aunt Ruth was the only one mom would listen to, so Carrie called and asked her to talk to mom. Aunt Ruth was able to finally convince her to go to the doctor. When she got there, the doctor found Gang Green in her leg. She stayed in the hospital for a while. I sat in my room not knowing what to think. I wondered how it came down to this. My friend told me people with diabetes are more prone to infections and that can make them extremely hard to treat. She said that even a minor cut can lead to a serious infection. "Did they tell your mom about this?" my friend asked. "No," I said. "I don't know what they told her. I never went with her to her appointments." I was so confused. Now they were saying she had to have her leg amputated and that if she didn't, the infection would eventually kill her. I looked at my friend and she said "You know, having this procedure done could save her life. It would stop the infection from spreading anywhere else." "I know," I said. "She'll be glad to be out of pain." I thought this would be the end of it but little did I know, the worst was yet to come.

COPING WITH CANCER

A few days after surgery, she was fine and ready to go home. I was glad that everything went well with the surgery. She told us she wasn't going to stop doing for herself until she had no choice. Mom was stubborn but I really wished she would just get some rest. After a while, they started her with therapy. She had to learn how to use a prosthetic leg. I was so proud to call her mom. She was a true legend to me and always would be. I wish you could've seen her throughout the years and how she never let anything stop her or get her down. It was truly amazing. She would keep us updated instead of herself. We just wanted to make sure she understood the major change her body just went through. We moved to a bigger place in Dalzell. I started to notice mom would say and do certain things that just weren't in her character to do. I would always go in Barbara's room and tell her what mom was saying. I was a little worried. We didn't think much about it after that.

I started watching the most beautiful baby I become to love; Kaitelyn. That's when dad started getting sick. He stopped eating and soon after he stopped drinking as well. He looked like a different person. He was dropping weight like crazy. He'd lay in bed and wasn't able to get up for a while. Seeing him like this brought tears to my eyes but I'd had enough. No more tears for me. I went into my room and prayed for my dad hoping he would get better. I had just lost my grandma and aunt not too long ago. All I wanted him to do was get better. When I prayed, I believed as well. My family was in denial but not me. I just prayed and believed. All of them kept telling mom what to do and how to do it. Instead of telling her what to do, we should have come together as a team, support each other, and pray together for dad. Instead some were worrying about life insurance, dad's car, and his TV. Those weren't even irrelevant at a time like this. When they admitted my dad one of my brother's went to the hospital and asked him a stupid question. No one wants to be questioned when they fear that there life is close to an end. After he asked that, dad was upset. He wasn't happy at all. I don't blame him. I would've been mad too.

Some family members called dad's sisters to come see him thinking he was going to die. I didn't know what was going on. Things were just getting out of hand. What was wrong with us? If the doctors didn't say anything bad, why were we saying things like we knew what was going to happen? The only person who knew when it'd be his time to go was God. When they used to say negative things I would walk away. Some days in my room, I'm not going to lie, I used to think the worst about dad's condition but then I would turn my mind back positive.

Dad was diagnosed with bone cancer. Luckily, the kind he had was treatable. He had it for so many years. I see why he didn't want his family to know anything about him. Look at the way they reacted. Mom had told us about dad. We knew for a while dad had this but we didn't say anything about it. We weren't supposed to know anyways. We didn't think anything of it because he was looked fine and healthy. My dad is the only boy in his family, so he never really had a brother. He did so much to care for his family and that's all that mattered to him. He may not have carried us in his womb but the pressure of taking care of so many did him the same way as mom. He suffered too. He never left her side and he stood there through the hard times. I used to love when he sung with us. We were like the Jackson 5 but only there were more of us. Back in the day dad loved his afros and working on his cars. Everyone used to say he was the meanest man on earth but truth is he didn't like being around many people. My brothers were scared of him and the girls knew how far to go with him. He loved to look at wrestling, just like his mother, and still does. Looking at him, he reminds me of his mom. When I lost my grandma she left a piece of her for us to have forever; her son, and I will never forget that. I know he misses her just as much as we do. I wanted to know more on his condition and what could happen since everyone was saying there were different stages of this cancer. Now I know he's fine. I still wanted to learn about it so I looked deeper into it.

I found that there are many types of cancer that are able to metastasize to the bones. The most common types of cancer that spread to the bones are arising from lymphatic to blood cells. Lymphoma and multiple myeloma can also frequently affect the bones. My dad has multiple myeloma and this is for those that don't know what type of cancer this is. I looked farther to see about this disease and what could be done because looking at my dad, he was suffering. That hurt me. No one would want to see their loved ones like this. Killer diseases; this is what I will be studying in the future. His condition is curable thank God. Multiple myeloma, this cancer begins in your cells. New cells form when the body doesn't need them causing the old, damaged cells to not die when they should. The extra cells can form a mass of tissue called a growth or tumor. In time, myeloma cells collect in the bone marrow. This may damage the solid part of the bone. The myeloma cells collect in several of your bones. This is why the disease is called multiple myeloma. This disease can cause harm to your tissues and organs, such as the kidneys.

I was happy when he started to go to the doctors more often because he was showing signs of improvement. He was beginning to be his self again. I know we all have to leave this earth someday but God wasn't ready to take him yet. If you could've seen my dad you would have said the same thing. Learning about this stuff changed my life and my family's as well. Some of us were worrying about the side effects of the treatments he was receiving. Others were worried about how to fit this into their everyday lives. The reason I think this was so hard for us to deal with was because we had no kind of communication within the family. Nobody knew how to come together and deal with it as a family. You have to pay attention to each other, the signs could be there. After many months of going to get treatments, dad came home one day. Mom and I were in the kitchen talking when he walked towards us. I left out to use the bathroom. When I came back mom told me to call around and tell them dad went into remission. I was so happy. I hugged my sister first and told her. She was happy too. We both said "See, God will make a way out of no way." Everyone was shocked. Dad was cooking again, doing the yard, and taking mom places. Every once in a while he'd get sick, but it's nothing like he use to.

Mom took good care of her family. Nobody could say she didn't. The warnings she gave to us, her love and her courage held the tree we stood under. Her prayers and brave heart are what gave her such a great big family, all because she believed. Her hands stayed folded and eyes opened towards heaven. There's no one like her. Now she was facing the worst struggle in her life.

HER FINAL STRUGGLE

One day my sister and I were sitting on the porch with mom and the wind was blowing. It felt good having a nice family time, joking around. There were people building homes around us. Mom started talking asking do you yall remember this person or that person? and we were like "No mom, not at all." Then we laughed. I said to her "You're going too far back," and then my oldest sister yelled "Oh yea, I remember now. Sure do." Well I didn't. I said "These people you knew weren't around when I was born." "No you right," said mom. Then she started to say some stuff that left me and my sister wondering like huh? Later on that night she wasn't feeling good. Four days later, she still wasn't feeling good so she decided to go to the hospital. That's when they admitted her to the hospital. They didn't really know what was going on with her. Then you had people calling asking what's going on with mom. I wanted to yell "I don't know myself wait and see then everyone will know!!!" Now mom had been back and forth in the hospital. Some times were longer than others. We tried to help her the best way we could because we didn't want her thinking we were plotting on her. After seeing events that took place in my home I knew something was wrong! What it was? I don't know. I'm not a doctor and at the same time everyone was confused asking what was going on with her. I didn't want to tell them because I didn't want to scare them. I didn't want them to take things and turn it around to something totally different from what I told them. Yea, it's just that crazy.

I've only seen my mom cry twice in my life and it hurt me so bad. It made me feel like I was the bad guy. I did a research on some of the things that were happening. When I did, it brought up all these different types of diseases. The main one it talked about with those symptoms was Alzheimer's disease. We didn't know what she had. This is something we looked into because she couldn't remember things.

This disease has a big family to it and secondary it occurs because of the disease or injury some researchers believed. They did autopsies on the brain showing up to 45 percent of people with dementia had signs of both Alzheimer's and vascular disease. This disease has many symptoms including decreased intellectual functioning. It interferes with their normal life. It goes on to describe them to have 2 or more major life functions impaired or lost such as memories and also language. Other impaired functions include perception, even judgment, and reasoning. They may lose emotional and behavioral control and can develop personality changes. They can have problems solving and abilities can be reduced or even lost. There are so many different classification schemes for dementia. They can have certain things happen to them. Please look out for clues like this:

- cortical-memory, language, thinking, social withdrawal

- subcortical-emotions, movement, memory

- progressive-cognitive, abilities, worsen, overtime primary-result from a specific disease primary-result from a specific disease.

I'm not saying this is what she had but I knew what I saw every day. I talked with my sisters about it and saw what they had to say about it. One of them showed me some papers she printed out about it. I took it and read it. It was saying how a person with this disease would think someone was in the room with them but really it'd be their shadow. Sometimes she thought she wasn't home so her doctor did the test on her. The results came back and he said she doesn't have Alzheimer's or Dementia, she has depression. I was confused because all this I looked up was what my mom was doing. I didn't know what to believe and dementia has 7 stages of decline:

- Stage 1.no impairment

- Stage 2.very mild decline

- Stage 3.mild decline

- Stage 4.moderately decline

- Stage 5.moderately severe decline

- Stage 6.severe decline

- Stage 7.very severe decline.

Ask your doctor about things like this. It's better to be safe than sorry. It could happen to anyone. We never thought something like this would happen to our mother but now we knew. Now is the time to sit with your family and discuss things. We felt alone. Dad and I were the only ones that saw the everyday changes in mom. The things she said would hurt but you knew it wasn't her speaking. It was something with her mind, something we couldn't put our hands on since her doctor couldn't answer my question. I was trying to put my own theory together. Mom was 72 now and I knew at this age anything could happen to her, especially diseases based on family history. I missed my mom and the way things used to be. Seeing her in this stage of her life made it hard to come to terms with.

No one was prepared for things to happen this way. Sitting in the room with her one day I turned the TV. Something caught my attention and I wanted to check it out so I stayed on that channel. Looking at Keyshia Cole and Toya Wright's show was so touching. They struggled with trying to get their families together and do right by each other without fighting; something I could relate to. Their pain touched me in a way I just can't explain. I even cried watching their shows. This let me know we're not the only ones like this and it's ok to talk about it. All they wanted was to be a family. I forgot I was in the room with mom. It's a good thing she was asleep because dad had to step out to get some things from the store. I wished I could open up and express how I feel but no one would listen. I knew we loved each other but we never supported each other. I wish we'd get together and take trips, vacations, or just have everybody in one place for the holidays.

My dad always did so much and that's the side people never saw of him. He does have a soft side when it came to my mom. When she was sick, he made sure she was taken care of no matter what he had to do for her. That's the side I was so proud of. Even though he was sick himself, his main concern was my mom. These past couple of months put a strain on him but he managed to get through even the toughest of times. Although 2012 hit the hardest point in our lives, we were still happy both of our parents were here with us. There may not be any doctors, lawyers, judges, and actors in my family but one thing people knew was mom had many children and they all could sing. That's all we did growing up. Every church we went to knew my mom loved singing. She didn't only sing in church. She sang just about anywhere. She wasn't afraid or ashamed to open her mouth and praise God.

As the years go by, all I want to know is why? Why couldn't we all get together and do right by each other? I missed all the fun times. Even if I had a family of my own I would still want to get with my sisters and brothers to spend time together and have fun. I guess I'm the only one that sees this. The only time we really get together is when there's a death in the family and it shouldn't be that way but no family is perfect. I just miss the bond we had and the time we spent together. Some say we had it rough, and we did but mom was teaching us how to be adults and to never depend on a man or woman to take care of us. Her teaching brought us a long way. It helped us with making the right decisions in our life. She showed us to set goals for ourselves and always put God first in all things. Have faith and pray in all you do and your cup will be filled with joy. Mom and dad showed nothing but love and poured their hearts out to many. Even after raising 21 children, she still helped raise some of her grandchildren. She never had a break. She remained humble, tended to our needs, and helped take care of her brothers and her sisters when needed. After everything she did you'd think we would appreciate it and do the same for them both but I guess I was wrong. We do things thinking its ok but nothing is ok when you can't do the things you know you should for the ones that took their time to raise you and keep you protected and safe. Maybe one day we'll learn to do right by each other and our parents.

TO MY READERS

I just wanted to share these memories and the love of our family and the ones who came and touched our lives. I see these other families on TV with so many kids. One thing I can say is God blessed my family and I. Going to so many different schools and churches, meeting new faces, and dealing with issues took a lot out of us. Mom was right there with open arms letting us know that we may have to go through trials and tribulations but your final reward is well worth it. I hope that I touched someone and helped someone who went through anything we went through. Know that no matter what your family does to you, they're still your family and you still need to love them. Ask God to help you forgive them and never hold a grudge. The guilt will eat you alive if that person was to die. Life is too short. Enjoy it and make the best of it.

I would like to say thank you to God first and then to my parents Sally & John Witherspoon. My sisters and brothers; if it weren't for you I wouldn't be able to write this book. You all have shown me so much. To my nieces and nephews: Asjhia, Jabreia, Aleshia, Lapreia, Tyleshia, Brittany, Brandon, Tyler, Taylor, Jaeshon, Jaquann, DaeDae, RayRay, Nae Nae, AJ, Aaron, Sharlaine, Miya, Nicole, Trevor, Lil Arthur, Javon, Jason, Jermaine, Tarshia, Issac, John, Deion, Marcus, Dominique, Alexis, Tamika, Londynn, Brooke-Lynn, Jaylah, Lil Mackey, Raeana, Rayven, Cheronika, Lil Sam, Malcolm, Desomond, Shymeka, Betty, Daniel, Dajon, Tyreke, Steve, and Stephanie. Know that I love you and if I left anyone out, I love you as well.

ABOUT THE AUTHOR

As I was finishing this book my mom passed away August 25, 2012. This was such a sad day. I cried when I got the news and laid my head in her bed. I cried so many tears my eyes swelled. She wanted me to go on with the book so she could read it. It hurts so much that she won't get to do just that. My tears now are tears of happiness. She's in a better place. She's not in any pain and her suffering is long gone. I just wanted her to see me do something with my life. Now we've laid her beautiful soul to rest and if she's looking down I ask her to watch over me and guide me. I don't really know where to go from here. I'm scared to make another step because she won't be there to guide me through it. She was a strong woman and she gave birth to me so I know I will be just fine. I ask that you keep my family in prayer as we heal through this process. I still have a dad who needs us and we still need him. The holidays won't be the same without her. She's gone to heaven. I love you mom, I did it.